To: Bar

MW01491402

From: Marcus Taylor

COURAGE
TO OVERCOME

Finding Faith to Face Your Challenges and Win!

MARCUS C. TAYLOR

Brownstone Publications, LLC
Bloomington, Illinois

Published by
Brownstone Publications, LLC
P.O. Box 115 - Bloomington, IL 61702-0115
Printed in U.S.A.

Brownstone Publications, LLC is a Christian-based publishing company purposed to produce excellent quality books and other products that will advance God's kingdom in the earth. We are committed to partnering with Christian leaders, teachers, and business personnel to nurture and publish biblically-based ideas, market their message, and distribute it around the world.

Publisher's note: Brownstone Publications' publishing style capitalizes certain pronouns in Scriptures that refer to the Father, Son, and Holy Spirit, and may differ from other Bible publisher's styles.

Take note that the name satan and related names are not capitalized. We choose not to acknowledge him, even to the point of violating grammatical rules.
All emphasis in the Scripture quotations is the author's.

All scripture quotations, unless otherwise indicated, are taken from the New King James Version, Copyright © 1982, by Thomas Nelson, Inc. Used by permission. All rights reserved.

Details in some of the stories have been modified to protect the identities of the persons involved.

Cover Design by Brownstone Publications, LLC
Editing by Cassie Hart
Cover Photography by Rashod Taylor Photography

Acknowledgements

I want to thank God. I love Him for saving me
and for choosing me for His purpose. I am so
grateful to God. He gave me the desire to be a
writer. I know it was a part of His plan for my life
because He doesn't make mistakes. This book is
a part of my destiny.

I thank God that He gave me great parents to
watch over me. Mom and Dad, you are my
example of faith. I would not be who I am today
without you. Thank you for encouraging me to
accomplish my dreams and for celebrating with
me when I reach my goals. Thank you for
keeping me safe from danger and for showing me
the difference between right and wrong. Thank
you for speaking God's Word into my life. Now I
can be a godly man and withstand any
adversities that come my way.

Thank you for guiding the steps I take on my
journey to destiny. You build me up like no other
parent I know. You even catch me when I am

doing something wrong and show me a better way. You have never hurt me, nor have you abandoned me. You embrace me when I am down and out and you always show me love, the way God intended. I love you very much and I am glad God made me your son!

To Rashod, thank you for standing by my side and for sticking up for me. Thank you for taking pictures for my book cover. I pray that God will bless your diligence in photography and that He will open doors for you to go around the world.

To my little sister Krystal, thank you for encouraging me to stay strong and for believing in me. I pray that God will use you to do great things for His kingdom. I love you!

To Chequita, my big sister in the Lord. Thank you for having my back and for editing my chapters. Patience can make great things come to pass.

Love,
Marcus C. Taylor

COURAGE
TO <u>OVERCOME</u>

**Finding Faith to Face Your
Challenges and Win!**

MARCUS C. TAYLOR

Brownstone Publications, LLC
Bloomington, Illinois

Contents

Forward ....…..... 11

Introduction ....…. 19

1. Courage to be Chosen.............…..........…..... 23

2. Courage to be Transformed 31

3. Courage to be an Example 39

4. Courage to Pray 47

5. Courage to Try Again! 57

6. Courage to Believe When You Don't See 65

   About the Author ....…....................…...... 73

Forward

arcus Christopher Taylor is our second child, the middle child of our three children. This alone makes Marcus special. But it took some time for Desetra and I to realize just how special he was. Sometime after college, I worked at a local school named Sarah Raymond School. Sarah Raymond offered education programs and related services to children with special needs. My job required me to work with severely delayed students who were unable to care for themselves. Working with these children planted a seed of fear within me. I desired, as do most parents, to have healthy children; happy and active children with ten fingers and ten toes. I wanted my children to grow up having both the natural and spiritual ability to deal with such a cruel world. But God had a different idea. On January 12, 1990 Marcus was born. He was our beautiful baby boy!

Initially, we didn't know Marcus had special needs. It wasn't until he was almost two years old that we noticed significant changes. My wife was concerned, so we scheduled a developmental assessment for Marcus. After several visits and procedures, we realized our son had special needs. We will never forget the time Marcus was assessed by a developmental therapist—he was almost three years old at the time. The therapist gave Marcus a seemly simple assignment. He had to take a string and thread it through three large beads. He picked up the string in one hand and the bead in another. Marcus began to move his hands as if he was actually threading the bead, but the bead fell on the table. With a puzzled look on his face, he picked the bead up and attempted the task again, but the bead hit the table. Each time he tried to complete the task, the same thing happened—the bead fell on the table. Marcus just sat there with a confused look on his face. He couldn't figure out

We believe his condition was never given a name because God already defined him as being gifted.

what was wrong. It was at that moment we knew this was serious. Tears filled my wife's eyes. She stood there wondering if this was a dream and hoping we would wake up and it would all be over. But it wasn't a dream. This was our life and we had to face it. Desetra and I were heartbroken. As a parent, this type of situation causes you to feel like a failure, wishing you could do something to make things better, but you can't. It's totally out of your control. We couldn't help but think of our oldest son, Rashod, who was active and alert. He played sports and loved to run. On the other hand, we had a son who was "different" (as the world would call it). Marcus wasn't as active as Rashod, nor did he play sports at the time. Instead of enjoying time on the football field, my wife and I were trying to understand our three-year-old son, who could barely squeeze a ball.

It was through this experience that we learned firsthand what it means when God's Word says, "My grace is sufficient for you, for My strength is made perfect in weakness." (2 Corinthians 12:9) We had no idea what was ahead of us. Our only option was to trust that God would strengthen us for the process. The funny thing about the entire situation was that they could never really pinpoint what was wrong with Marcus. Though he had some characteristics of an autistic child, the

What we once viewed as somewhat of a failure or disappointment has now become a blessing—Marcus is our hero!

doctors never diagnosed him as autistic. His condition was undefined. No titles, no diagnosis. He was just Marcus. We believe his condition was never given a name because God already defined him as being gifted. There is no doubt in our minds that our son is gifted and anointed of God. Over the years we have watched Marcus persevere. He has overcome many challenges that have blown our minds. And to see how far he has come—especially to the point of writing this book—fills our hearts with joy. We have seen him walk through this process by faith. In fact, Marcus spoke this book into existence. Everywhere he went, Marcus talked about his book and how God was going to use it to encourage people. Our son worked hard to make this happen, putting forth effort on a daily basis. God has anointed him for this task and this book you are holding is evidence.

Marcus is a spiritual man, and he has a real relationship with the Lord. He prays for things and God answers. Many of you who know Marcus can attest that he, at some point in time, may have given you a word of encouragement from the Lord. We can even remember a few times when Marcus would minister to his high school teachers. They would ask us, "How does he know what we were feeling?" "Who told him?" Our only response would be: "God! The boy is gifted."

Marcus even makes a point to send encouraging messages through text. Our son literally has a texting ministry. It doesn't matter who you are: family, a friend, a classmate, a church member, if Marcus has your number, he will pray for you and send you a text because he simply believes the Word of God. He is a man of integrity; greatly used of the Lord. And we believe that one day our son will preach the gospel of Jesus Christ, and we will all be amazed at what God will release through him.

We have since come to realize that sports aren't everything. In fact, our oldest son eventually stopped playing football. He's now a professional photographer. So, it's not athletic ability that makes a good son—it's the spirit of God. Marcus may never reach the athletic status a father often desires for a son, but he has something greater than I ever could have imagined. He has an anointing from God! It is evident through all the challenges he has faced and conquered over the years.

God has truly graced our son with the courage to endure. There is nothing he can't do when he put his faith in action. He believes God, which is something we all can stand to learn how to do. We love Marcus dearly and we're so proud to be his parents. What we once viewed as somewhat of a failure or disappointment has now become a blessing—Marcus is our hero.

So, as you read our son's book, we believe you will be inspired. But understand this: just like Marcus found the courage to overcome, you too can find the courage *you* need to overcome. So we challenge you to grab hold of the message in this book. Begin to trust God for your next level. If He can empower our special needs son to overcome challenges, He shall do the same for you. As you believe, God will move you toward greater things in life and give you the Courage to Overcome!

Bishop Larry & Desetra Taylor

Introduction

Courage to Overcome

T he idea of writing a book never crossed my mind until one Friday night in November of 2008 when Apostle Leon Emerson spoke a powerful word into my life. My father, Bishop Larry Taylor, invited Apostle Emerson to our church as a guest speaker. During a three-night revival, Apostle Emerson ministered God's Word, and we were encouraged. On the last night of the revival, Apostle Emerson called me up to the front of the church. He began to speak to me, asking if I had a desire to write. He proceeded to say that "God has placed His word in my mouth" and God is going to "use me to write a book, specifically on the subject of overcoming struggles." In addition to writing, he said "I would become a voice for those who are physically challenged or who have been identified as having a disability."

I was very encouraged when Apostle Emerson

spoke these words. And I easily received his words because he confirmed what I had already accepted as truth. You see, ever since I was a small boy, my mom shared God's desire to use me for His glory. She would say, "Marcus, you are a man of God. You will speak God's word and lives will be changed. There is nothing

There are many things in life that can *disable* us, but why allow that to happen when we serve a God who is well able?

you can't do when God empowers you to do it." I knew writing this book would not be an easy task, but I believed I could do it. God said I would do it, and He cannot lie. He is God! Numbers 23:19 says:

> *God is not a man, that He should lie, nor a son of man, that He should repent. Has He said, and will He not do? Or has He spoken, and will He not make it good?*

This verse tells me that God would never go against His word. He is faithful! I was confident that His word would not return void. God had come through for my family and for me in times past. Everything God had spoken about my family to date had come to pass. Over the years, He has given us many victory trophies, so we have learned what it means to trust Him. When I began to remember the many victories God had given me, my heart was filled with courage to tackle this new challenge.

Although I hadn't written a long paper before, I was committed to the process of writing this book. That night, I began jotting down ideas and notes about various challenges I had personally overcome. I worked on completing my book daily, diligently writing chapter after chapter. I was so excited about this project that I began sharing my ideas with the members of my church, even though I wasn't finished writing.

Each time I sat down to write God would remind me of a different challenge I had overcome. I thought about my challenges in school, how I was misunderstood and teased, and even the anger I felt at times. These trials were once real in my life, but with the help of God and my parents I learned from my experiences. Though it was hard, God strengthened my faith to face them. I didn't know at that time that God was empowering me to overcome adversity so that my life would be an example of victory for someone else.

I believe that I can inspire you to live abundantly through my testimonies of victory. Be determined to erase the doubts of the enemy and fully hold on to what God has spoken to you. There are many things in life that can *disable* us, but why allow that to happen when we serve a God who is well able?

You are more than a conquer through Christ who strengthens you. My life is an example of how you can do anything you set out to accomplish. This book is my proof! I pray that you will receive strength today and that you will realize God is with you. There is no obstacle too big that will block your path to destiny. After reading about my struggles and the steps that I took to overcome them you, too, will be motivated to find the *Courage to Overcome.*

Marcus C. Taylor

Chapter One
Courage to Be Chosen

You did not choose Me, but I chose you and appointed you that you should go and bear fruit, and that your fruit should remain, that whatever you ask the Father in My name He may give you.
John 15:16

It feels good to be used by God. I become excited when He leads me to pray for someone or when He tells me to encourage someone. I feel joy in my heart when I do these small tasks. I know God could use someone else—there are people who are stronger, smarter, and older than me. Some have been Christians longer and have more experience than I do. But instead God chose me. He decided to use me to share the gospel of Jesus Christ and to encourage His people. I didn't know why God decided to choose me. My dad says, "God uses ordinary people to do extraordinary things." I believe that's me! It does not make sense by man's way of thinking. But God does not see as man sees. He does not think as man thinks. He did not choose me for

my natural abilities and outer appearance. He
chose me for what is inside me—His Word!

IT'S ON THE INSIDE!

As a small child, it was evident that there was
something special about me. My mom would
say, "Marcus, you are special to God. You will be
greatly used by Him one day." I didn't fully
understand the power in my mom's words at the
time. I would simply smile and receive the words
in my heart. I did not realize God had shared my
purpose for life with my mom. He was using her
to impart purpose within me. Her words gave
strength to His Word on the inside of me.
Jeremiah 1:4-5 says:

> Then the word of the LORD came to me,
> saying: "Before I formed you in the womb
> I knew you; before you were born I
> sanctified you; I ordained you a prophet
> to the nations."

God knew me before I was born; His Word
shaped me while I was in the womb and it
sanctified me for the special call on my life.

FRUSTRATED BY THE CALL

Having a special call did not free me from having challenges in life. I still had to overcome many obstacles. For example, sometimes it is difficult for me to stay focus, so learning new things is a challenge. This has always been a difficult task for me, especially when I was in grade school. I did not take regular classes like everyone else did; it took longer for me to learn subjects like math and English. At first I didn't understand why things were harder for me. On the outside I was much like my schoolmates: we were close in age and height, and some of us were in the same grade. Yet what was easy for others did not always come easy to me, and I would become frustrated. "Why can't I do what others my age are able to do?" I'd ask. My mom would see my frustration. She would remind me of God's Word inside me and mention His special call on my life. She would encourage me to be confident in who God

> **I could rely on God to strengthen me to do all the tasks I couldn't do on my own. I had a personal relationship with God.**

created me to be. My mom helped me to see that there were only a *few* things I could not do, but *several* things I was able to do that my schoolmates couldn't. I could hear from God. I could speak God's Word and situations would change. I could pray and God would hear me. I could encourage my teachers and classmates to live holy before the Lord. I could rely on God to strengthen me to do all the tasks I couldn't do on my own. I had a personal relationship with God.

I saw that the enemy was using frustration to discourage me. Eventually I stopped focusing on what other people were able to do and the hurtful things they said. Instead, I focused on what God said about me. I began to believe He would give me everything I needed to succeed, and that He would equip me to reach my destiny.

I believe God created me differently because He wanted me to stand out. God knew what abilities I should have and He created a plan for how they should be used. I believe He created you with special abilities also. You too can overcome your own frustration. Stop allowing the enemy to anger you. You don't have to focus on the tasks you can't do; instead, ask God to give you the courage and strength to accomplish the tasks you were created to do.

CHOSEN TO FACE A GIANT

One of my favorite stories in the bible is about David and Goliath. I like this story because David showed me how God gives us courage to do the tasks we were created to do. 1 Samuel 17 tells us that the Philistine army didn't like the children of Israel, so they decided to wage war against them. There was a Philistine giant named Goliath who was over nine feet tall and wore full armor. Every day Goliath came to the battle site to challenge the Israelites to fight. King Saul and the whole army were afraid of Goliath.

But David wasn't afraid. He told Saul, I, "Your servant will go and fight him." Saul was not confident in David's abilities. He thought David was too small and too weak; that he was just a kid. He told David, "You are not able to go out against this Philistine and fight him; you are only a boy." However, David did not let his size or age

27

stop him from completing the task. David knew he was chosen. And he knew God would strengthen him to defeat the giant in his way.

David did not use Saul's armor or sword; he chose to face the giant with his shepherd's staff, five smooth stones, and a slingshot. I Samuel 17:45-47 says:

> Then David said to the Philistine, "You come to me with a sword, with a spear, and with a javelin. But I come to you in the name of the LORD of hosts, the God of the armies of Israel, whom you have defied. This day the LORD will deliver you into my hand, and I will strike you and take your head from you. And this day I will give the carcasses of the camp of the Philistines to the birds of the air and the wild beasts of the earth, that all the earth may know that there is a God in Israel. Then all this assembly shall know that the LORD does not save with sword and spear; for the battle *is* the LORD's, and He will give you into our hands."

David was chosen by God to face Goliath. He didn't let his own frustration or other people's negative thoughts stop him. He focused on God's thoughts about him. David received courage from God. He used the tools that gave him victory in the past and the skills God placed inside him to defeat Goliath. David was victorious because God chose him to defeat Goliath.

There are many things I can't do. But I now know I can do all the things God has chosen me to do. God has given me special abilities. He has also given you special abilities. I encourage you to use them for God's glory. Don't let others frustrate you. Trust that God will give you the courage and strength to defeat your personal giants. You were chosen to do so!

Chapter Two
Courage to Be Transformed

And do not be conformed to this world, but be transformed by the renewing of your mind, that you may prove what is that good and acceptable and perfect will of God.

Romans 12:2

I saw the movie *Transformers* when it first came to the theaters a few years ago. I loved this film! It was full of action and it was funny, but it had a positive message. It was about giant robots that were able to change into different types of machines like cars, trucks, and airplanes. Some of the robots were good and others were bad. But both had the power to transform into something else.

Like the robots in this movie, I believe I, too, have the power to transform. I don't mean change the way I look, but I can change how I think and act. God gave me the power to transform into the man He has called me to be. I am able to transform areas of my life by reading and walking in His Word daily. Change is not always easy, but it is possible. God's word gives us the power and courage to transform. Hebrews 4:12 says:

> For the word of God is living and powerful, and sharper than any two-edged sword, piercing even to the division of soul and spirit, and of joints and marrow, and is a discerner of the thoughts and intents of the heart.

God's Word is living. It is powerful! It is the force that empowers us to change. His Word is like a sharp sword that cuts away the sin in our life. God's Word shows us how to live as Christians, and it is the answer to the challenges we face daily. That's why God tells us to seek Him daily; He encourages us to come to Him for daily bread and instructions. When we seek God we find answers; we find everything we need to grow as Christians. Here are a few Scriptures that show us how God's Word can change our lives:

> Your word *is* a lamp to my feet and a light to my path.   Psalm 119:105

> Direct my steps by Your word, and let no

iniquity have dominion over me.

Psalm 119:133

Sanctify them through thy truth: thy word is truth.

John 17:17

He sent his **word**, and **heal**ed them, and delivered them from their destructions.

Psalm 107:20

This Book of the Law shall not depart from your mouth, but you shall meditate in it day and night, that you may observe to do according to all that is written in it. For then you will make your way prosperous, and then you will have good success.

Joshua 1:8

God's Word can transform us in many ways. Through daily devotion we can renew our minds. If we change our thinking, then we can change the things we do. I know this because God's Word has changed me. My mind is renewed daily by His Word. God has cut things out of my life that didn't give Him glory. That is why I believe being a Christian is the best thing that has ever happened to me. I know I would not be who I am today without God's Word in my life. I now have confidence in God and the faith to stand against tricks of the enemy. I have the power to live a transformed life!

TRANSFORMED DAILY

It's hard to live a transformed life without God. As a Christian, receiving Christ in our hearts is the beginning of our change. But we can't stop there. We have to present our bodies as a living sacrifice each day in the presence of God, praying and reading the Word. Daily devotion is good for us; it helps us to transform. Devotional time strengthens our walk with God so that we grow closer to Him.

> **I believe God has given us the power to transform our lives, and that this transformation begins with the word of God.**

When we are away from God's Word we become spiritually weak. At first we seem to be okay, but very soon we begin to die spiritually. It's like

34

jumping off a cliff without a safety net. The act seems fun for a moment, but eventually we will hit the ground hard and possibly, die. The enemy wants us to believe we are okay without God. He wants us to find pleasure in the "fun" sin offers. He never shows us the end result, which is (spiritual) death. This is how he entangles us in sin. But daily prayer and devotion can keep us from doing things we may later regret; it gives us the power to live a pure and holy life before God. It gives us the courage to stand against sin.

Many people may not know this, but I use to struggle with anger. I would get so frustrated and angry that I would want to fight. I can remember a few times when my brother, Rashod, would upset me. I didn't like being told what to do. When I felt like Rashod was bossing me around, I would become angry. In my rage, I would try to fight Rashod by swinging at him. This happened a few times. My father told me my behavior was wrong; that it wasn't godly. I knew I had to change. I was not pleasing God with my actions, so I prayed and asked God to help me. I even asked my parents to help me—and I read the

Word of God. Today I know what it means to be angry, and I can avoid giving in to sinful actions. I can now better control my anger with God's Word. I no longer try to fight my brother because I know that Rashod loves me. He is the oldest and I should obey him. Worldly thinking says, "Don't let anyone boss you around." But I don't have to conform to worldly thinking. I am a child of God and He says to "present my body as a living sacrifice" (Romans 12:1). He says, "Obey those who rule over you" (Hebrews 13:17). God's power transformed this area of my life. He used His word and my parents' guidance to help me and now I'm no longer entangled in this bondage.

TRANSFORMATION IS GOD'S WILL

We all desire God's will for our lives. But to fully walk in His will we must be transformed. When God transforms us, He changes us from the *old* and into the *new*. But it's a process! We have to do something different in order to be transformed. Ephesians 4:22-24 says:

> ...that you *put off*, concerning your former conduct, the old man which grows corrupt

according to the deceitful lusts, and *be renewed* (transformed) in the spirit of your mind, and that you *put on* the new man which was created according to God, in true righteousness and holiness (emphasis mine).

When I struggled with anger I had to ask for help from God and from my parents. Then I had to stop the behavior that made me want to fight. I also had be obedient to those gave me instructions. That is how my life was transformed.

I believe God has given us the power to transform our lives, and that this transformation begins with the Word of God. Daily prayer and devotion is the key to living a transformed life. It can help keep us from doing or saying things we might regret, or that will not be pleasing to God. In His presence is where we find strength to change and to overcome challenges we face daily. His Word tells us that we can make it. If we fall in the process, we don't have to give up. God knows how to use His Word to transform our failures into victories.

Chapter Three
Courage to Be An Example

Let no man despise thy youth; but be thou an example of the believers, in word, in conversation, in charity, in spirit, in faith, in purity.

1 Timothy 4:12

God has chosen me to be an example. Everywhere I go—school, church, and work—I try to live a life that is pleasing to God. But it's not always easy living as an example for others. It takes courage because there is always someone watching to see how I handle different situations. Some people offer encouragement and others do not, but I don't let the thoughts or actions of others keep me from being an example. Instead, I focus on how I can walk out God's Word because I am chosen.

God chose me to be an example of a believer before I was born. He even placed me in a Christian home and chose my parents. He knew they would be able to raise me according to His

Word. I have great parents; they are an example of faith. My father is the senior pastor of Center for Hope Ministries. He is a man with vision, and God uses him to speak words of faith into people's lives. Both my dad and mom have shared the gospel in other nations. People around the world call them for spiritual and natural advice. They desire to have the favor and anointing of God

> **Being a Christian requires us to represent Christ at all times, so our actions must be Christ-centered.**

that rest on my parents. My dad tells us often, "God called us (my mom and dad) to be an example." They didn't always know how God was going to use their life, but God did. My parents have strong faith in God and they are not afraid to obey Him. That is why our family is blessed; my parents are willing to follow God all the way, and so am I. My parents have taught me how to live by faith and how to stand for God. They taught me that living for God is the best way to go through life. When we follow God, He can get glory from our lives and His light can shine through us. This is how the Lord uses me, for I, too, am an example.

When I was in high school, one of my special education classes was a work-study program where the teachers prepared us to work real jobs in the community. Through this program I was able to get a job at a local nursing home. I was excited about my job. God wanted to use me as an example for the other workers and the elderly people who lived there. Two years later, I still work at the nursing home and I love it. I know God blessed me with this job because He wanted to use me for His glory. I represent His light in the midst of darkness. Whenever I go to work, I am an example of faith for those who are faithless. God gives me words of encouragement to share with the other workers, and my words have power. I believe the people at my job are changing for the better because of my godly example.

God calls on us to be an example in our love toward us others, but this is not always an easy task. I can remember a time when I was sharing my faith with a friend at school. I explained to him God's love and His desire for us to be Christians. He didn't want to hear about God because He didn't believe God was real. He said to me, "There isn't a God." He rejected God's love and chose not to accept Christ into his heart. I was angry with him; I didn't want to talk to him again. I even began to ignore him, but I felt bad. I wasn't acting like a Christian. I decided to show him unconditional love because that is what Jesus would do. Loving people unconditionally is challenging, especially when they do not show love to you in return. But their behavior should not change how you act toward them. Christ shows love to us even when we don't deserve His love. He expects us to follow His example by showing love to others, even when we feel they do not deserve it. God's Word tells us to "love your neighbor as yourself" (Mark 12:31). I would never ignore myself, so I couldn't ignore my classmate. Instead, I chose to be an example of God's love. I didn't talk with him about God as much, but I continued to pray for him. I showed him love through my actions and godly examples. My actions were strong enough to show him that God was real.

SOME MAY NOT FOLLOW

We are faced with choices every day—choices that can either connect us to God or pull us away from our destiny. But through it all, we have to remember that we are chosen to be an example. As a Christian, being an example is not a choice; our only choice is to either be a good example or a bad one. Being a Christian requires us to represent Christ at all times, so our actions must be Christ-centered. Everywhere we go, someone is always looking. Someone may be watching

We must devote ourselves to following Christ even if our peers don't follow our example.

to see if God is real in our life. That's why we must devote ourselves to following Christ even if our peers don't follow our example.

In Numbers 13, the Bible talks about Joshua and Caleb, who were leaders under Moses. They were different from other leaders because they had a heart to follow God all the way. I believe Joshua and Caleb were examples. People were always watching them. When the children of

Israel were afraid to possess the land God promised, Joshua and Caleb encouraged them to believe God. Numbers 14:6-9 says:

> But Joshua the son of Nun and Caleb the son of Jephunneh, *who were* among those who had spied out the land, tore their clothes; and they spoke to all the congregation of the children of Israel, saying: "The land we passed through to spy out *is* an exceedingly good land. If the LORD delights in us, then He will bring us into this land and give it to us, 'a land which flows with milk and honey.' Only do not rebel against the LORD, nor fear the people of the land, for they *are* our bread; their protection has departed from them, and the LORD *is* with us. Do not fear them."

Joshua and Caleb believed God. They were an example of faithfulness and devotion to God. But the others did not follow their example and they were punished. God did not allow the Israelites over age twenty to enter the Promised

Land. God rejected them because of their disobedience, and He declared that they would die in the wilderness. Only Joshua and Caleb would have a chance to dwell in the land.

There are rewards for us when we are examples of faith. God honors us. He is looking for us to live godly lives so that others will have a reference point for His character. When we are godly examples, we are living as a true disciple of Christ. That's why we must follow Him with our whole heart. 1 Peter 2:21 says, "For to this you were called, because Christ also suffered for us, leaving us an example, that you should follow His steps." When we follow Christ, he gives us the ability to endure and the courage to stand firm. There are many things that I can't do, but I don't let it stop me. I try to follow God with my whole heart, and God rewards me for my devotion by giving me the strength to overcome and the power to do things I never imagined.

While it can be hard to be an example, I believe that with God it is possible. We can make a choice to walk out God's Word. Some may follow and some won't, but we can't focus on that. Instead, focus on God. He chose us to be His example so He will give us the ability to walk it out. We never know when someone is watching to see if God is real. It may be someone at work or at school. It could be a visitor at church. No matter who it is, God has given us the power to change the lives of everyone we meet. We are examples of the believers. So let's act like it at all times!

Chapter Four

Courage to Pray

Therefore I say to you, whatever things you ask when you pray, believe that you receive them, and you will have them.

Mark 11:22-24

I have always believed in the power of prayer. When I was a child my parents taught me how to pray in faith and believe that God would answer my prayers. I have prayed for many people, some good and some bad, and have seen the results of my prayers many times. I pray every day, and I have faith that God will answer my prayers.

Prayer gives me joy because I know God answers prayers. Prayer changes things. The sick can be healed and the backslider can return to God. That's why we must pray for everyone—not just family members and friends—but everyone. And we must pray always. One time is not enough. I Thessalonians 5:17 says, "Pray without ceasing" and Colossians 4:3 tells us to "Continue earnestly in prayer." Prayer is powerful. When we pray continually, God promises to answer us.

GOD WANTS TO HEAR OUR PRAYERS

Prayer is an important part of our Christian walk. It is a time to connect with God. It's an opportunity to talk with Him and listen as He reveals His plans for our life. It's a good feeling when God answers our prayers. It motivates us to pray more because we know the Lord hears us. The more we pray, the more we will recognize His voice, and the easier it is for God to direct our life. When we seek the Lord we can find the courage to live as true followers of Christ. We can grow in confidence knowing He hears us and that He will answer us. God's Word tells us:

But without faith *it is* impossible to please *Him,* for he who comes to God must believe that He is, and *that* He is a rewarder of those who diligently seek Him.

Hebrews 11:6

The righteous **cry** out, and the LORD **hears**,

and delivers them out of all their troubles.

Psalm 34:17

I waited patiently for the LORD; and He
inclined to me, and heard my cry.

Psalm 40:1

God rewards us when we diligently seek Him.
Prayer exposes our weakness and it shows God
how much we really need Him. God is always
listening for our cry. He desires for us to call on
Him for strength, courage, peace, or for whatever
else we need. That is why I pray every day. I
know I can boldly go before His throne and find
the grace to help me in my time of need
(Hebrews 4:16).

FAITH TO BELIEVE

It takes courage to pray in faith. We have to
believe, without doubting, that we will receive
what we are asking God to do. James 1:6-8
says:

But let him ask in faith, with no doubting,
for he who doubts is like a wave of the

49

sea driven and tossed by the wind. For let not that man suppose that he will receive anything from the Lord; *he is* a double-minded man, unstable in all his ways.

> **Prayer gives us the faith to believe and the courage to overcome.**

Doubt has the power to kill our faith. It can even hinder our answers from God. When we doubt, we are not confident in God's ability to answer our prayers. That is why we must have courage when we pray. We can't allow fear and doubt to weaken our confidence in God no matter what challenges appear before us. Prayer is the key; it will give us the power to triumph over the enemy.

I remember a time when God led my family to pray for one of my mom's friends. The doctors found a tumor in her spinal cord and they said she would never walk again. We began to pray, and one day God spoke to me and said, "This is just a test. My healing power is coming your way. Have faith! She will walk again." My mom's friend was in a wheelchair when God spoke these words to me. It did not look like she would walk again; she truly needed a miracle. But I did not waver; I was confident in God. I shared the message with my mom and she told her friend. This gave her faith to believe in God, and today she is walking! She no longer needs a wheelchair and she does not use crutches. God answered our prayer and He gave my mom's friend a miracle.

God used this situation to strengthen our faith and to show us how to pray at another level. This challenge taught us how to pray. Many people do not like challenges, but they have a purpose: to strengthen our prayer life. God made us conquers; His Word says we are overcomers. If we never experience challenges, how can we be called overcomers? Challenges lead us to prayer. When we pray, we find strength to withstand the attacks of the enemy and the courage to "fight the good fight of faith." Then we are able to see that we can overcome everything satan throws at us. We learn that there is a greater strength on the inside of us: Jesus Christ! We are encouraged to believe God even when tempted to yield to fleshly desires. This is how we become conquers, and how we use prayer to overcome!

PRAYER THAT CREATES NEW DOORS

Our prayers are powerful. They give us the ability to bring things into existence that were not there before. That's why we don't have to fear when things don't turn out the way we hope or plan. Prayer changes things; it opens doors. There are two scriptures that always

We receive power to speak against everything that is not of God and to declare open doors in our lives and in the lives of others.

encourage me to take my own challenges to God in prayer. They are:

Be anxious for nothing, but in everything by prayer and supplication, with thanksgiving, let your requests be made known to God; and the peace of God, which surpasses all understanding, will guard your hearts and minds through Christ Jesus.

Philippians 4:6-7

Ask, and it will be given to you; seek, and you will find; knock, and it will be opened to you. For everyone who asks receives, and he who seeks finds, and to him who knocks it will be opened.

Matthew 7:7-8

I don't worry about anything, but I pray about everything. Anything I desire God to do, I pray about. I have seen many doors open through the power of prayer. One of those doors opened about a year ago. When I was a senior in high school I told my parents I wanted to attend college. My brother was away at Murray State University, so I thought it would be cool for me to attend college, too. I began telling people I would soon be a college student. I told my classmates, teachers, and even some of the members at my church. Many people didn't believe this was possible. I use to struggle with schoolwork when I was high school, plus I was enrolled in special education classes. And at the time Heartland Community College didn't have any courses to fit my needs, but that didn't matter. I still believed I would go to college, so I kept praying.

After I graduated from high school, I talked with my parents again about attending college. Still there were no doors open for students with special needs. I continued to work at the nursing home—but I didn't stop praying. I believed my prayers would open a door for me to become a college student.

In January of 2009, my mom decided to contact Heartland Community College to see if there were classes available for me. One of the counselors shared information with my mom about a new program called HALO (Heartland Academy for Learning Opportunities). The HALO program is a two-year program created for people with disabilities and special needs. The counselor also told my mom the program was new and that it would begin in the fall. She thought I would be a great candidate for the HALO program and recommended that I enroll for the next school year. When my mom gave me the news, I was so excited. God heard my prayer and He answered me. God's Word is true; the "...effective, fervent prayer of a righteous man avails much." (James 5:16) When classes began

in the fall I was a student at Heartland
Community College. On my first day of classes I
noticed the buildings were much bigger than my
high school. I said to myself, "Wow, this is a big
school!" Another student helped me find my
classes and bought me some doughnuts. I sat in
my class and ate doughnuts while the teacher
was talking. I was grateful to God. I had the
courage to pray and the faith to believe. God
answered my prayer!

I believe God has called us to pray. Prayer gives
us the faith to believe and the courage to
overcome. Prayer gives us the strength to fight
the good fight of faith and to become warriors of
God. We receive power to speak against
everything that is not of God and to declare open
doors in our lives and in the lives of others. I
know that I am a prayer warrior and I believe you
are, too. Now, let's pray together:

*I pray that the man or woman reading this
book will find the courage to pray and faith
to believe that You will answer their
prayers. I pray that they will have patience*

to wait on You. Lord, give them an ear to hear when You speak. I pray that their prayers will give them strength to withstand the devices and deceptions of the satan. Release Your anointing upon them right now, and destroy all bondages that hinder their faith. Take their prayer life to another level. Give them courage to step outside their comfort zone and into their destiny so they can show forth who Jesus Christ really is. In Jesus' name, Amen!

Chapter Five

Courage to Try Again!

For a just man falleth seven times, and riseth up again: but the wicked shall fall into mischief

Proverbs 24:16

Basketball is one of my favorite sports. When I play I go at it hard, especially against my dad and my brother. I play with all my might because I want to win the game. Winning means a lot to me. It makes me feel like a real conqueror. I do not like to lose. Losing feels bad, especially when playing against my dad in basketball. Sometimes I even get frustrated because I know I can beat him. I have seen my brother win a few games against him, so I know it is possible. Every time I lose I'd say, "One more game, Dad. One more game." Most times he quits. I know that if I continue to try, eventually I will win. I have the courage to face this challenge no matter how many times I lose. I believe one day, if I keep trying, I will win.

In this world, we all have challenges to face. We have all failed at something or have made mistakes along the way. Sometimes disappointments and embarrassment keep us from trying again. But if we just believe in God, He can give us the courage we need to try again. Sometimes we think that being a Christian will save us from failure. It doesn't! But with Christ in our life, we can overcome all obstacles and challenges, even the ones we have failed at before. Proverbs 24:16 says, "...a just man falleth seven times, and riseth up again...." We need courage to try again. We need faith to believe again. Faith is not staying down; it is getting up. When we trust God we can be confident that He will give us courage to get back up. I know. I have tried to accomplish many tasks and have failed. I have felt the sadness and embarrassment of having to do something again and again—only to fail. But God has been with me throughout all of my struggles. I have learned not to dwell on my disappointments for too long. Instead, I focus on what I need to accomplish and then I try again. I don't try again fearing failure. I try in faith, believing that God will give me the ability to do what I desire to do.

Many people know I have special needs. Though I can't always do what everyone else does, I am stilling willing to try. I don't allow anyone to tell me "Marcus, you can't." That is a lie. I can! God's Word says in Philippians 4:13, "I can do all things through Christ who strengthens me." So I believe God will give me the strength to do what I must for His kingdom.

FAITH THAT OVERCOMES

Victory is mine and defeat has no place in my life.

Once my dad preached a message called "Faith to Overcome the World." I enjoyed this sermon because it showed me that I am more than a conqueror through Christ Jesus. In his message he said, "You don't have to be afraid of the enemy. You are an overcomer. Christ has overcome the world and if you are born of God, you have the same authority. You can overcome the enemy with faith." When my dad spoke these words, I was encouraged. I don't have to fear. I don't have to be a failure. I can walk in faith. Our enemy, satan, is always working to discourage the believer. He wants us to believe we are defeated, but he is a liar. We can't believe anything he says. We must only believe God's word.

I remember a time when satan tried to discourage me. I desire to drive a car one day. Everyone in my family has a car except me, and I believe I should have one too. If I had a car I could get to work, school, and church on time. I don't like having others drive me around all the time. So I have been praying for God to bless me with a car. But I don't want just any car; I want a Mustang. This is my desire and I believe it will happen for me. But first, I need to get my driver's license.

> **The enemy will use our disappointments and failures to keep us down, and pressure can kill your spirit. But God's Word can give you life.**

I didn't get a chance to take Driver's Ed like my brother and sister. I had to take special education classes instead when I was in high school. If I had taken Driver's Ed, I could have received a driver's permit. Now I have to take a written test at the DMV. My dad gave me a copy of the "Rules of the Road" so I could study for the test. When I finally had a chance to take the test, I was confident that I was going to pass. But I failed! I was upset because I failed the test. I was embarrassed. I had told everyone I was going to get my permit. Now they would see my failures. The enemy wanted me to believe that I was defeated; he wanted me to give up on my dream of owning my car and driving on my own. But I didn't give up. I failed the test, but I was not defeated. My dad encouraged me. He told me, "Son, you can take the test again; next time study harder." So, I decided to try again. I began studying for the test. I even took a practice test to see if I understood the questions. The time came for me to take the test again, and I failed.

I could not believe it. I studied very hard this time and I still failed the test. I was very sad. Now I was beginning to doubt if I could pass the test. But my faith would not let me give up. My faith made me believe that I was more than a conqueror through Christ Jesus. I began to remember all the times God had been there for me. He has seen me through every struggle in my life and He will see me through this one. I decided to stand firm on my faith. I will continue to go after my desires no matter what, and I will do it with confidence. Victory is mine and defeat has no place in my life. I believe I will celebrate victory everywhere I go and in everything I do. God made me a winner!

God made you a winner too. You may have failed or you have made some mistakes in the past. You can receive courage from God. Get back up. Try again. Stop focusing on past failures and mistakes. You can't change the past, but you can focus on what's ahead. Philippians 3:14-14 says, "Brethren, I do not count myself to have apprehended; but one thing I do, forgetting those things which are behind and reaching forward to those things which are ahead, I press toward the goal for the prize of the upward call of God in Christ Jesus." This is not the time to throw in the towel. Get back up again. You have to encourage yourself with God's Word. The enemy will use our disappointments and failures to keep us down, and pressure to kill our spirit. But God's Word can give us life. When I failed my driving test the second time, I was upset, but I could not remain angry. I could not focus on my failure; I could only focus on what was in front of me. I would soon have another chance to try again. I could not let the fear of my past failure distract me from preparing for the future. I believed there was something greater in store for me than what I was feeling at the time. So as I write this book, I am preparing to take the test again. Next time, I will be ready. I shall pass my test and receive my driving permit.

We will have struggles in life. We will fail and make some mistakes. But we must never give up. We must continue to try. God is with us. He never leaves us in the fire alone. If it is His will, it shall come to pass. Don't lose your faith in the process; only believe. When you find the courage to believe you will begin to see your desires. God did it for me and He will do it for you, but you have to find the courage to try again!

Chapter Six

Courage to Believe
When You Don't See

Jesus said to him, "Thomas, because you have seen Me, you have believed. Blessed are those who have not seen and yet have believed."

John 20:29

I have faith in the things that seem impossible to man. If God said it, then I believe it. But sometimes believing in what I cannot see is hard. Sometimes the enemy tries to sow seeds of doubt in attempt to weaken my faith. But I don't let him. Instead, I fight back. I read the Word of God. I receive strength through prayer. I talk to my parents. I do what I have to because I can't let the enemy steal my faith. I don't want to miss out on my future because of doubt and unbelief. I fight because God gave me the power to win.

Having power to win will not stop the enemy from fighting against us. Ephesians 6:12 says, "For we do not wrestle against flesh and blood, but against principalities, against powers, against the rulers of the darkness of this age, against spiritual *hosts* of wickedness in the heavenly *places."* The enemy is not fighting us with guns and knives. He uses discouragement, fear, and doubt as weapons against the people of God. When doubt enters our hearts, fear and unbelief follow. We become confused and our faith in God grows weak. Without faith we cannot please the Lord, and the enemy will win. Instead of doubting, now is the time to strengthen our faith. We must not waver at God's promises for our life. We have to hold on, even when we cannot see the answers clearly.

When I was a freshman in high school my mom said to me, "Marcus, I believe you will sing in the choir." I didn't believe it. I didn't want to sing in the choir. But my mom really believed I would. Every few months, she would say, "Marcus, are you ready to join the choir?" And each time, I would say, "No, Mom! I'm not joining the choir." She eventually stopped asking. After I graduated from high school, I felt the Lord leading me to join the choir. I talked with my parents and we set up a meeting with the choir director. Today, I am a member of my church choir and I like it a lot. God revealed to my mother the plan He had for me. Though I didn't see it at the time, my doubt didn't stop it from happening because my mom believed it would. She had faith and she held on to what God had spoken to her spirit. When God has plans, nothing, not even doubt, can stop it.

SHIELDED BY FAITH

Faith is our shield against the enemy. It protects us when the enemy throws unbelief at us. Ephesians 6:16-17 says, "Above all, taking the shield of faith with which you will be able to quench all the fiery darts of the wicked one... And the sword of the Spirit, which is the word of God."

The enemy tries to frustrate us with distractions and discouragement in hopes of making us doubt God.

We have to use our faith and the Word of God because these are the weapons God gave us to use against the enemy. Faith and God's Word work together; this is how we build our faith. Romans 10:17 says, "So then faith cometh by hearing, and hearing by the word of God." I receive faith through God's Word.

This is why I read and pray daily, and I listen to different messages because they also feed my faith. One of my favorite preachers is T.D. Jakes. He is an anointed man of God. The word that God gives Bishop Jakes always ministers to me. It strengthens my

> **We have to believe that everything God has spoken over our life shall come to pass. All we have to do is believe!**

faith to stand against the enemy. I have been watching T.D. Jakes since I was in grade school. Every morning I would get up and watch his show, *The Potter's House*, at 6:00 a.m. before getting ready for school. The show doesn't come on in the morning anymore, so I watch it on Sunday evening. To this day I still buy his DVD series because his ministry has blessed my life. T.D. Jakes' message motivates me to think beyond my past and gives me hope for the future, even when I don't see it. This is why I am willing to buy sermons that will feed my faith. I do this because I desire to grow and God's Word gives me faith to believe for all things. Listening to messages and reading God's Word helps me to

fight the good fight of faith. It helps me to stand firm because one day I will also preach the gospel. God has anointed me to share His Word just like my father. I have a passion for God's Word and He placed it inside me so that I can minister healing to the hurting and freedom to those who are bound all over the world.
Watching men of God like my dad and T.D. Jakes inspires me to live right so that God can use my life. It gives me courage to believe in God. If He can bless their ministry, God will do the same for me. But I have to believe. I can never doubt. I must stand on what I know is true—and that is the Word of God.

We all are believing God for something. Whatever it is, it will come by faith. We have to trust God knowing that "He who has begun a good work in you will complete it." (Philippians 1:6) He is faithful!

FAITH TO STAND FIRM!
It is safe to stand on the Word of God. It's a solid foundation. But after waiting a long time for the promise, sometimes our faith can get weak. The

enemy tries to frustrate us with distractions and discouragement in hopes of making us doubt God. That is why we have to stand firm on God's Word. We must hold on and believe even when we do not see. God is faithful! He cannot lie. Numbers 23:19 says,

> God *is* not a man, that He should lie, nor a son of man, that He should repent. Has He said, and will He not do? Or has He spoken, and will He not make it good?

When God says things about our lives He expects us to believe it. We must trust God and not try to fix things ourselves. Abraham and Sarah made this mistake. In Genesis 15, God told Abraham that he would give him a son with his wife. The bible said in verse six that Abraham "...believed in the Lord..." Abraham believed at first, but then he started to doubt because he had to wait a long time. Abraham and Sarah decided to do things on their own. Abraham had sex with their maidservant Hagar and they had a son named Ishmael. But Ishmael was not the promise God spoke about; he was not a part of

God's plan. And so Abraham and Sarah paid a price because they did not wait on God.

I am going to wait on God. I desire the promises God has for me. I am praying and my family is praying for me so that I won't compromise. My dad teaches us that God's way is the best way and I believe him. So, I must walk in holiness. One day I desire to be married. Right now I am a single young man, but I plan to be married one day. I see the love my parents share and it makes me smile because they have a great marriage. I watch how my father loves and cares for my mom and think, "One day I shall have the same thing." But I have to wait on God's timing. I can't afford to mess up. I must have a woman of God because she will bring favor to my life. Proverbs 18:22 says, "*He who* finds a wife finds a good *thing,* and obtains favor from the LORD." So I am believing that God will bless me with a wife; a woman who believes Christ as her Lord and Savior. She has to be a woman who loves the Word of God as I do and who enjoys having devotional time with the Lord; a woman who desires an intimate relationship with God that includes daily prayer and seeking God's face for our family. I have shared these desires with my mother. She said, "Son, you can have what you desire if it lines up with the will of God. You shall see it come to pass." Though I do not see it right now, I still believe. I shall wait on God.

It takes courage to believe God when you don't see the promise. It's easier to just try to make it happen on your own. But when we do, we step outside God's plan for our life. We have to believe that everything God has spoken over our life shall come to pass. All we have to do is believe!

About the Author

Marcus Taylor is man who knows how to connect to the heart of God. The son of a senior pastor, Marcus learned at an early age what it means to serve the Lord. He attends Center For Hope Ministries, where he serves as a member of the Voices of Hope Choir. His passion for God's Word often inspires him to share his faith with others. Marcus is know for the encouraging words he shares via text messaging to help young men and women strengthen their relationship with God.

Despite being born with developmental delays and characteristics of autism, Marcus has persevered through life's challenges with the power of God and the strength of his faith. "I'm not afraid to trust God!" are the words Marcus speaks to himself to fuel his faith for the impossible. One of his noteworthy acts of faith resulted from a desire to attend college. After several years of academic struggles, many believed Marcus would not be a suitable candidate for college. But Marcus believed he would not only attend college, but that he would graduate. In the spring of 2011, he will participate in the first inaugural class of the HAL0 (Heartland Academics for Learning Opportunities) program at Heartland Community College.

Marcus is without a doubt an inspiration to all. His life is a reminder that having a disability is not an excuse to distrust God's ability to empower us. We can accomplish all things when we allow God to strengthen us for the task.

Marcus is a native of Bloomington, Illinois. He currently lives with his parents, Larry & Desetra Taylor, and his siblings, Rashod and Krystal.

CPSIA information can be obtained
at www.ICGtesting.com
Printed in the USA
JSHW081229030423
39830JS00002B/110

9 780983 005537